Take a trip to
JAPAN

Text and photographs by
Gwynneth Ashby

General Editor
Henry Pluckrose

Franklin Watts
London New York Sydney Toronto

Words about Japan

archery

bean paste

Beppu

Boys' Festival

Buddhist temple

'bullet trains'

Fuji-san

Emperor

Empress

geta

Girls' Festival

Honshu

Inland Sea

incense smoke

Hokkaido

kimono

kendo

Kyoto

Kyushu

Nara

rice

rice fields

scroll painting

seaweed

shrines

tatami

tea ceremony

Tokyo

yen

Yokohama

Franklin Watts Limited
8 Cork Street
London W1

SBN UK edition: 85166 863 1
SBN US edition: 0 531 00990 4
Library of Congress Catalog Card No:
80 52719
© Franklin Watts Limited 1980

Printed in England by
E T Heron & Co Ltd, Silver End, Witham, Essex

The author and publisher would like to
thank the following for kind permission to
reproduce photographs: International
Society for Education Information Inc.
(page 21); Japan Information Centre
(pages 9, 29 and 30); Japan National
Tourist Organisation (pages 20 and 31);
Mitsukoshi (UK) Limited (page 13);
Jonathan Rutland (page 7).

Maps by Brian and Constance Dear.

Most Japanese children go to nursery school when they are about three years old. Children start school when they are six. The new school year begins in April.

The children help give out the
school lunch. They wear white
masks so that they will not breathe
germs over the food. Anyone with a
cold wears a mask to school.

4

Young school children usually wear yellow hats. The main roads are busy. The drivers watch out for the children in their hats.

This picture shows some Japanese
stamps and money. Japanese money
is called yen. There are coins and
notes.

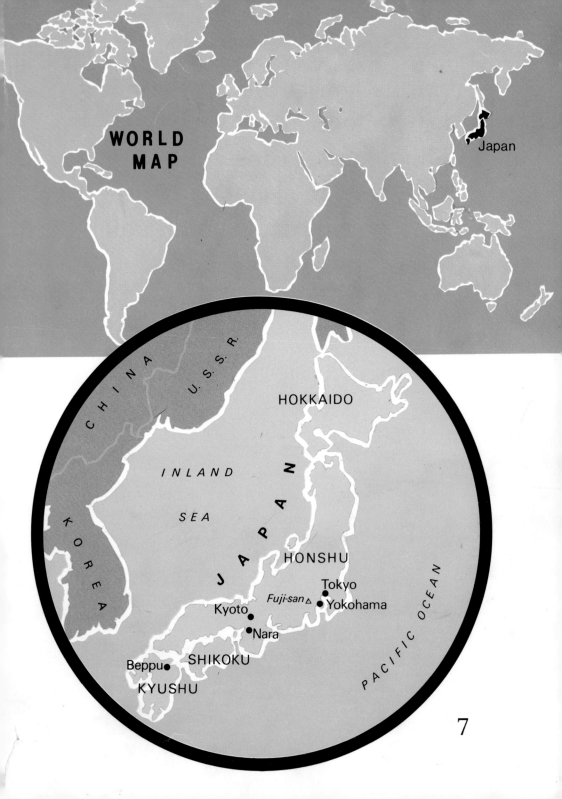

WORLD MAP

Japan

CHINA

U.S.S.R.

HOKKAIDO

INLAND

SEA

KOREA

J
A
P
A
N

HONSHU

Tokyo

Fuji-san △ ● Yokohama

Kyoto ●

Nara ●

SHIKOKU

PACIFIC OCEAN

Beppu ●

KYUSHU

7

Many houses are built of wood. The windows are protected by sliding doors. People take off their shoes when they enter a house. They leave the shoes in a small entrance hall.

The floors of a Japanese home are
covered with mats, called tatami.
Tatami are made from a type of
grass. The national dress is called
the kimono. It is worn on special
occasions, such as the New Year.

In the evening a Japanese family has a hot bath. A cover keeps the water hot. First, each person washes and rinses off the soap outside the bath. Then they can enjoy the clean bath water.

Japanese people eat a lot of rice.
They also eat a fish soup mixed with
bean paste. The Japanese often eat
specially-prepared seaweed.
Sometimes the seaweed is put in
soup and sometimes it is mixed with
other dishes.

The Boys' Festival is on 5 May. Most houses display model armour. The plastic fish at the side are carp. Live carp are very brave. Japanese parents hope their sons will be as brave as the carp.

The Girls' Festival of Dolls is on 3 March. These are special dolls. The girls do not play with them. Emperor and Empress dolls are displayed on the top shelf. Then there are the court ladies, musicians, guards and servants.

Tokyo, the capital of Japan, is on the island of Honshu. There are many busy stores and skyscraper blocks. Each district has a police box. A map on the outside of the box shows the streets and houses of the district.

14

Tokyo has hundreds of small streets, too. The curtains with the writing tell people what the shop sells. At the snack bar with the red lantern people can eat Chinese noodles and dumplings. The Japanese often eat Chinese food.

Japan has four large islands and hundreds of smaller ones. The islands have many good ports.

Yokohama, near Tokyo, is Japan's largest port.

Japanese people pray at Buddhist temples. Sometimes they rub incense smoke over their skin. They believe this will purify them before they enter the temple. Souvenir stalls sell gifts for people to take home.

The deer in the park at Nara are
very tame. Every evening the
deer-keeper blows a French horn.
The deer come in from the forest and
are shut up for the night in pens.
Nara was once the capital of Japan.

18

Kyoto was also the capital once.
Kyoto has many shrines. People buy
pieces of paper with fortunes written
on them. 'Bad luck' papers are tied
to a tree so that the bad luck will
fly away.

19

The Japanese often attend a tea ceremony. The tea is green and powdered. The water is boiled in an iron pot over a charcoal fire. People eat sweet cakes during the tea ceremony.

Puppet shows are very popular.
The puppets' heads are carved from
wood. The chief puppeteer wears a
kimono. The other puppeteers are
dressed in black. They wear black
masks with slits for the eyes.

During the summer children visit fairs. They like to catch goldfish. The children have a bowl and a scoop. The bottom of the scoop is made of rice-paper. Anyone who catches more than ten fish can keep two of them.

Archery is a popular Japanese sport. The bow is very long. Kendo is a form of fencing using bamboo swords. Each fencer wears a mask over his face, and a thick, padded coat to protect his body.

The Japanese often buy their fish
live from a seawater tank. Some of
the fish is caught in the Inland Sea –
a stretch of water surrounded by
three of the largest islands.
Beppu is a port on the southern
island of Kyushu.

24

Several of the islands have volcanoes, which puff out smoke and fumes. In some places boiling springs bubble out of the ground. People can buy eggs cooked in the boiling waters of a pool.

Some people have a small workshop in their home. They make things such as fans, dolls and special clogs called geta. On the next page you can see someone wearing a pair of geta.

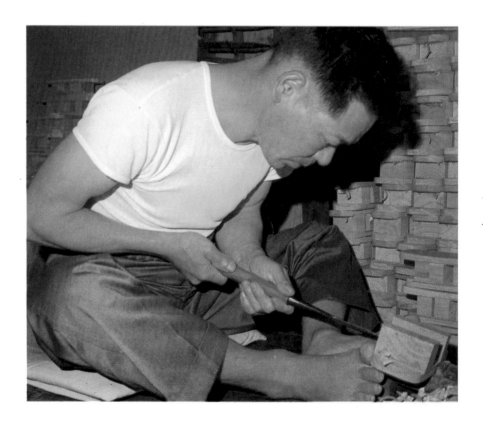

Busy crossings have a box of yellow flags on the edge of the road. Young children hold up a flag when they cross the road. The boy goes to senior high school. Most children in Japan wear uniform.

To celebrate some festivals, the Japanese make models from papier mâché. When the models have dried, they are painted. Slipper socks are put on the feet. The strap of a kimono sandal goes between the toes.

Rice is grown on most of the islands. Banks are built between the fields to keep in the water. The drawing is the symbol for a rice field. There are several thousand of these picture drawings.

In Japan there are many high-speed express trains, called 'bullet trains'. There are long windows on each side. This train is passing Fuji-san, Japan's highest mountain.

The islands of Japan stretch a long
way from north to south. The coldest
island is Hokkaido, in the north. In
winter there is a lot of snow. People
go ski-ing and skate on frozen lakes.

Index